Made in the USA
Monee, IL
14 August 2024

63900703R00057